Cambridge ICT Starters

Initial Steps

Third edition

Jill Jesson and Graham Peacock

CAMBRIDGE
UNIVERSITY PRESS

CAMBRIDGE
UNIVERSITY PRESS

4381/4 Ansari Road, Daryaganj, Delhi 110002, India

Cambridge University Press is part of the University of Cambridge.

It furthers the University's mission by disseminating knowledge in the pursuit of education, learning and research at the highest international levels of excellence.

www.cambridge.org
Information on this title: www.cambridge.org/9781107624993

© Cambridge University Press 2013

First published 2003
Second edition 2005
Third edition 2013

Printed in India by Shree Maitrey Printech Pvt. Ltd., Noida

A catalogue record for this publication is available from the British Library

ISBN 978-1-107-62499-3 Paperback

Additional resources for this publication at www.cambridgeindia.org

Cambridge University Press has no responsibility for the persistence or accuracy of URLs for external or third-party internet websites referred to in this publication, and does not guarantee that any content on such websites is, or will remain, accurate or appropriate. Information regarding prices, travel timetables, and other factual information given in this work is correct at the time of first printing but Cambridge University Press does not guarantee the accuracy of such information thereafter.

....

....

Every effort has been made to trace the owners of copyright material included in this book. The publishers would be grateful for any omissions brought to their notice for acknowledgement in future editions of the book.

Introduction

Cambridge ICT Starters: Initial Steps has been written to support learners who are following the Cambridge ICT Starters syllabus. It follows the syllabus closely and provides full coverage of all the modules. The sections of the book correspond to the modules and follow the order in which the modules appear in the syllabus. The book builds on keyboard skills and basic routines, such as emailing, handling data, basic spreadsheet management, creating and editing written work and handling images.

The book provides learners and their helpers with:

- examples of activities to do
- exercises for practice
- instruction in using their computers
- optional extension and challenge activities

It is designed for use in the classroom with coaching from trained teachers. Where possible the work has been set in real situations where the computer will be of direct use. The activities are fairly sophisticated yet simple enough to be followed by adults as well as children!

Some exercises require the learners to open prepared files for editing. These files are available to teachers on www.cambridgeindia.org website. The website provides useful graphics and templates for creating pictograms. Some pictures and text files are also included to help young learners so that they can learn editing without first creating the files required.

The activities in this book use Microsoft Office 2007 software, Paint, Wikipedia, Microsoft Outlook Express 2007 and MSWLogo. However, the syllabus does not specify any particular type of software in order to meet the learning objectives.

Please note that when learners view the screen shots contained in this book on their computer screens, all the type will be clearly legible.

Contents

INITIAL STEPS

Module 1 Starting with Text

1.1	Letters	2
1.2	Words	3
1.3	Capital letters	4
1.4	Sentences	6
1.5	Save	7
1.6	Writing poems	9
1.7	Changing a story	10
1.8	Selecting and changing	12
1.9	Editing	15
	Optional extension and challenge activities	18

Module 2 Starting Images

2.1	Paint	21
2.2	More tools	23
2.3	Duplicating images	25
2.4	Pictures from shapes	26
2.5	More skills	27
2.6	Editing pictures	29
	Optional extension and challenge activities	31

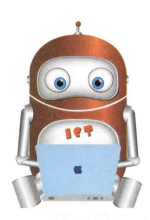

Module 3 Starting Graphs

3.1	Pictograms	34
3.2	Survey	36
3.3	Column chart	37
3.4	3-D column chart	40
3.5	Comparing charts	42
	Optional extension and challenge activities	44

Module 4 Starting Control

4.1	MSWLogo	46
4.2	More commands	49
4.3	Drawing pictures	50
4.4	Recording commands	52
	Optional extension and challenge activities	54

Module 5 Starting Searches

5.1	Using buttons and hotspots	57
5.2	Index and hyperlink	58
5.3	More searches	59
5.4	Keyword	60
5.5	Finding information	61
	Optional extension and challenge activities	63

Module 6 Starting Email

6.1	Email account	65
6.2	Replying	66
6.3	New message	67
6.4	Email folders	68
6.5	Forward and Cc	70
	Optional extension and challenge activities	72

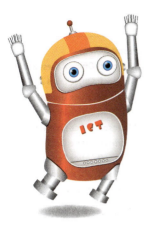

Module 1
Starting with Text

Learning Objectives

	Student is able to:	Pass/ Merit
1	Enter simple words using keyboard or other input devices	P
2	Select and edit text	P
3	Select basic icons (e.g. print, save or spellcheck) using the mouse	P
4	Name, save and retrieve documents	M
5	Use appropriate methods to check text is error free	M

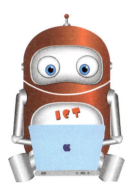

Start MS Word

- Click  to open the Start menu.
- Select ▶ **All Programs** .
- Select  **Microsoft Office Word 2007** .

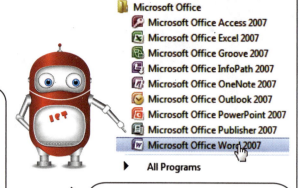

You can also start Microsoft Word by clicking the shortcut on the desktop of the computer. Look for the logo and the label Microsoft Office Word 2007  *.*

Open Microsoft Office Word 2007 by clicking here.

Letters on screen

- Tap the key  .
- You will see the small letter a on the screen.
- Tap  .
- If MS Word automatically changes a to A, it has been set to change the first letter of a sentence to a capital letter.
- Tap the letters sdfghjk and tap  . Only s changes to S.

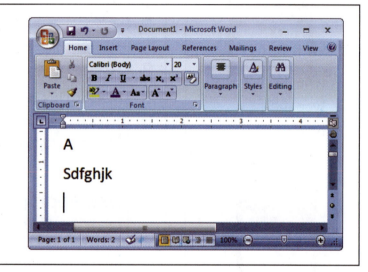

Delete

- Use the mouse to click the cursor I at the back of the last letter k.
- Tap once. The letter k is deleted.
- Tap until all the letters are deleted.
- Make a new list of 10 letters.
- Use the mouse to click the cursor I next to a letter in the middle of the list.
- Tap to delete the letter.
- What would you do if you wanted to delete all the letters?

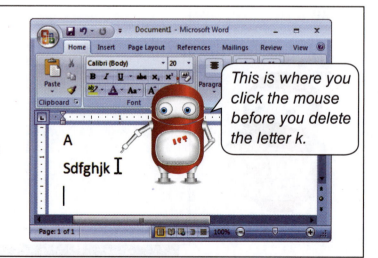

This is where you click the mouse before you delete the letter k.

1.2 Words

Type words

- Type these words:

  crash

  bang

  ping

- Tap 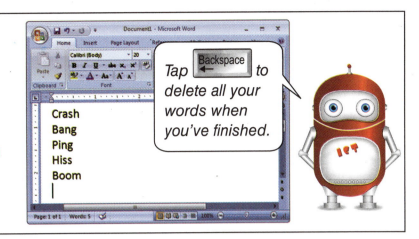 ↵Enter to start new lines.
- Add other noisy words like hiss, boom and tock.
- Add other adjectives like tall, good and fun.

Write your name

- Type your name.
- Type it four times.

- Tab Backspace ← to delete your name.

Make a list

- Type the name of a friend.
- Type the name of another friend.
- Type a list of five friends.

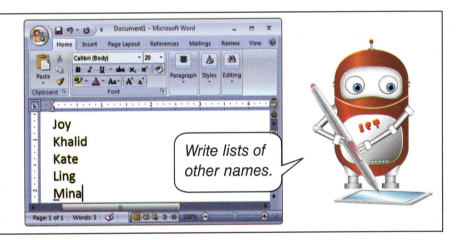

Make a number list

- Tap numbers and ↵Enter to make a number list.

Shift key

- Tap the key B.
- Hold ⇧Shift. Tap the letter again.
- This puts a capital letter on the screen.
- Tap ←Enter to start a new line.

- Put pairs of letters in a list.
  aA
  bB etc.
- Delete your pairs of letters.

Symbols

- Tap !1.
- Hold ⇧Shift and tap !1 again.
- Hold ⇧Shift and tap ?/ to get a question mark.
- Put pairs of numbers and symbols in a list.

- Delete your pairs.

When you hold ⇧Shift *, you get the symbol not the number.*

Caps Lock

- Tap Caps Lock.
- Look for the caps lock light on the keyboard.
- Tap Caps Lock again. The light goes off.
- Tap letters when the light is on. These will be capitals.
- Tap numbers with the light on. These are still numbers.

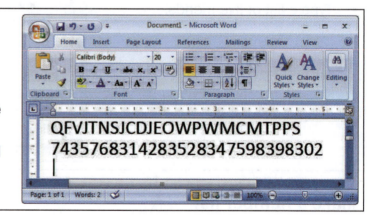

QFVJTNSJCDJEOWPWMCMTPPS
7435768314283528347598398302

Capital name

- Type your first name.
- Remember the capital to start.
- Tap the space bar.
- Type your family or second name.

My name is Metal Man.

Insert words

- Click in front of your name.
- Type *My name is*.
- Tap the space bar.

The new words push your name across the page.

My name is Metal Man.

TV names

- Make a list of your five favourite characters.

Use capital letters to start.

- Click the cursor I in front of the first line and tap ⏎ Enter 2 times.
- Move the cursor back to the first line.
- Type a title to the list.
- Call the list *Top Five TV*.

Top Five TV

Bart Simpson
Scooby Doo
Mickey Mouse
Bugs Bunny
Pink Panther

Places you know

- Type the name of the place where you live.
- Type the names of other places that you can visit.
- Put them in a list.
- Type a title at the top.

You can type cities or countries.

Places to go
Kuala Lumpur
China
United Arab Emirates
New York
New Zealand
London

Write a sentence

- Type this sentence: In my family there are children.
- Click in front of children.
- Type the number of children there are in your family.

Change the sentence to In my family there is one child *if you are the only child.*

Write another sentence

- Write another sentence:
  In my family there are pets.
- Type the number of pets you have.

How many pets do you have?

Write sentences

- Write sentences about you and your family.
- Use your own words.

Remember to add full stops at the end of sentences.

More writing

- Write about yourself by completing the following sentences:

  o My name is _____.

  o I am _____ years old.

  o I am a _____ (boy or girl?).

  o I live in _____.

  o I have _____ brothers and _____ sisters.

  o My pet is _____.

  o My favourite food is _____.

  o My favourite game is _____.

Try these sentences in your computer. Don't put a space before the full stop. Put the space after it.

Save

- Write a sentence about your house.
  My house has a nice garden.
- Ask your teacher to create a folder on the desktop of the computer for you (using your name) if you have not got one.
- Click  to save your work.
- Select your folder.
- Give your work a name you can easily remember (e.g. MMHouse) and click Save .

Use the drop-down box to select your folder.
My initials are MM, therefore I save my work as MMHouse.

Carry on working

- Write more sentences about your house.
- Every few minutes click 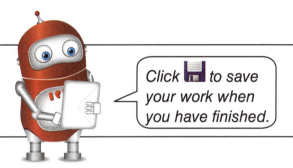 to save your work.

Click to save your work when you have finished.

A new piece of work

- Click to start a new piece of work.
- Write a sentence about a friend.
  My friend Asif has brown hair.
- Click after the sentence.
- Make sure you select your folder each time you are saving your work. Type MyFriend as the filename.
- Click Save .
- Write two more sentences.

Asif has two sisters.
My friend Asif is very nece.
- Click .

Type with the spelling mistake nece. You will learn how to correct it later.

Open your saved work

- Click .
- Choose the file you want to work on.
- Click Open or double-click the file to open it.

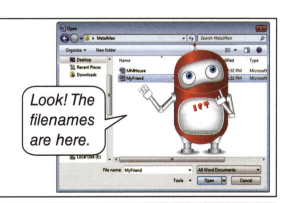

Look! The filenames are here.

Select text

- Click the cursor next to the word or the text you want to select and drag across it.

Double-click to select a word. Triple-click to select a line.

Add a big title

- Open the file MyFriend that you have saved in the previous exercise.
- Type a title on the top line.

My friend Asif

- Triple-click the title to select it.

Make sure it is highlighted!

Choose a number here to make the title bigger. The bigger the number, the larger the text size.

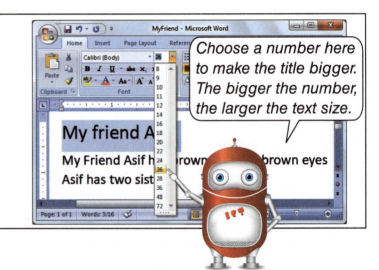

Checking spelling

- Click the Review tab.
- Click **ABC** ✓. This checks your spelling and find words that are spelt incorrectly.
- Some words like names are spelt correctly, but the computer doesn't know them. Click [Ignore All] if your spelling is correct.
- The word nece was detected as a spelling mistake.
- nice was highlighted as a suggested replacement.
- Click [Change] to accept and change.

Choose the best suggestion here.

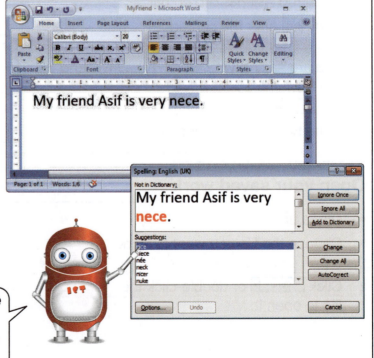

Counting rhyme

- Copy this poem:

Snake rhyme

One, two, three, four, five,
Once I caught a snake alive.
Six, seven, eight, nine, ten,
I let go of it again!

Tap ⬅ Enter *at the end of each line to move the cursor to a new line.*

Remember to use a capital letter at the start of a line.

Change the title

- Triple-click to select the title.

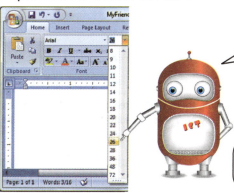

Click a number here to change the size of the title.

Click here to change the colour.

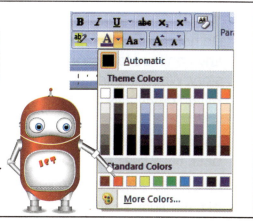

Align the title

- Triple-click to select the title.

- Click ≡ to align the title to the right.

- Click ≡ to align it back to the left.

- Click ≡ to align it to the middle.

Print preview

- Click 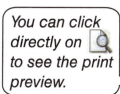 to open Office menu.

- Hover the cursor I over the  to see the 🔍 **Print Preview**.

You can click directly on 🔍 to see the print preview.

Snake rhyme

One, two, three, four, five,
Once I caught a snake alive.
Six, seven, eight, nine, ten,
I let go of it again!

Print preview shows what your work will look like when it is printed.

- Click 💾 to save your poem.

- Click 🖨 to print a copy of the poem.

Insert a word

- Here is the start of a story. Type it.

  Once upon a time there were bears.

  Click the cursor before the word bears and type three.

Auto word wrap

- Do not tap [← Enter]. Tap the space bar once and continue to type the next sentence of the story. When the line reaches the end, Word will automatically bring the cursor to the next line.

  Daddy bear was a bear. Mummy bear was a bear. Baby bear was a bear.

- Add these words as shown:

  big, medium, small.

Change a word

- Now add this sentence:

  They lived in a cave in the woods.

  Double-click the word cave to select it.

- Type the word house. This replaces the word cave.

Change another word

- Add this sentence:

  Mummy bear made some food.

- Double-click the word food.
- Change it to porridge.
- Look for another word: woods.
- Change it to jungle.

Add a big title

- Click in front of the first word Once and tap ⏎ Enter once.
- Move the cursor back to the first line.
- Type: The three bears.
- Tap ⏎ Enter .
- Triple-click to select the title.
- Click 12 ▾ to choose a number to make the title bigger (e.g. 28).
- Click and change the colour of the title to blue.
- Click 🔍 to preview the story.

The three bears
Once upon a time there were three bears. Daddy bear was a big bear. Mummy bear was a medium bear. Baby bear was a small bear. They lived in a house in the jungles. Mummy bear made some porridge.

Try different colours and sizes for the title.

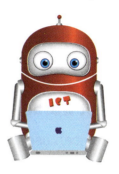

Save the story

- Add in the following lines to complete the story of the three bears.

  A girl called Goldilocks came to the house. She was hungry. She ate all the bears' porridge!

- Click 💾 to save the story when you've finished it.
- Give your work a name you can easily remember and click Save .

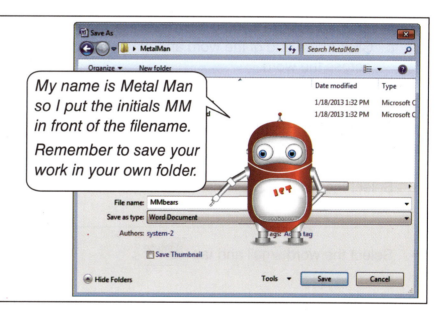

My name is Metal Man so I put the initials MM in front of the filename.

Remember to save your work in your own folder.

Another story

- Write a story about a monkey who loved cake.
- Write about how he stole cake from the kitchen and ran away with it. Write with your own words and try to make it interesting.
- Add a title.
- Click 💾 to save your work.

More sentences

- Type the following sentences:

She has two cute pets.

We have eight small beautiful

animals in our family.

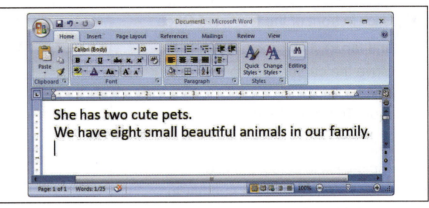

Select words

- You can use the mouse to select a word in three ways. Practise selecting a word:
  o Double-click the word. It becomes highlighted.
  o Click at the beginning of the word and drag across the word.
  o Click at the end of the word and drag across the word.

When you drag, hold the mouse button down.

Select a word and delete

Carry out the following instructions and write down your observation:

- Select the word cute and click .

_____

- Select the word small and tap 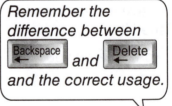.

_____

- Select the word beautiful and tap Backspace ←.

_____

Remember the difference between Backspace ← *and* Delete ← *and the correct usage.*

Select a word and change

- Select the word two.
- Type the word three.

two changes to three!

Move a word

- Type the following sentences.

  In my class there are sixteen girls and twenty boys. My family lives very close together to my best friend. We walk to school everyday.

- Select the word together and click ✂.
- Click the cursor I in front of the word everyday and click 📋.
- Can you exchange the word sixteen with the word twenty by using the above options?

Undo

- If you want to undo something, you can just click ↶.

- You can also just hold down Ctrl and tap Z.

Move a sentence

- Type the following story:

  Today is my birthday. I have invited many friends to my birthday party. We really are having fun all day! They give me a lot of presents. We play games, sing and enjoy eating the foods prepared by my mother.

- Select the sentence We really are having fun all day! and click ✂.
- Click the cursor I at the end of the paragraph, after the full stop.
- Click 📋.

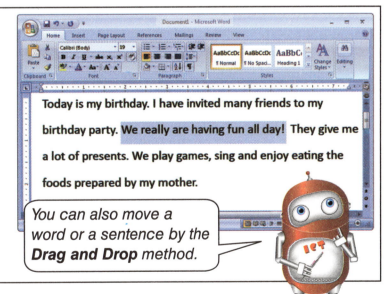

You can also move a word or a sentence by the **Drag and Drop** method.

Save and open your work

- Saving your work:
  - Click 🪟 to open Office menu.
  - Click 💾 Save As ▸.
  - Give your work a name you can easily remember and click Save.

- Don't forget to save in your own folder.
- Open the saved file:
  - Click 🪟 to open Office menu.
  - Click 📂 Open.
  - Select the file you want to open and click Open ▾.

Correct a sentence

- Look at this sentence.
- The word ridding was spelt wrongly and was crossed out. The correct word riding was shown in red.
- Can you find another mistake? Correct it using a red pen.
- Type the corrected sentence.

riding
I am ~~ridding~~ on my dike.

Jim's work

- Here is a story written by Jim.
- Copy his work.
- Don't change anything.

We went the market. i went with

my mum. we went on the bus. I

help mum to carry there bags.

They were very hevvy.

We went the market. I went with my mum. We went on the bus. I helpt mum to carry there bags. They were very hevvy.

Marked work

- Read these changes.

We went to the market. I ~~i~~ went with

my mum. ~~we~~ We went on the bus. I

helped ~~helpt~~ mum to carry ~~there~~ the bags.

They were very ~~hevvy~~ heavy.

- Double-click to select the words that are wrong.
- Type the correct words.
- Save your work using a suitable filename.

It's easier to change your work on a computer than on paper!

Dina's work

- Here is a story written by Dina.
- Click ☐ to start a new document.
- Copy Dina's work exactly.
- Don't change anything.
- Save the file as Dina's story.

I went to an old house with my frind Sara.

There was no one in the hosue. We

pushed The door. It opened. The house

was smally. There were spiders

everywhere. We herd Sounds from the

kitchen. What was it.

Marked work

- Read the changes Dina's teacher made.

I went to an old house with my ~~friend~~ **friend** Sara.

There was no one in the ~~hosue~~ **house**. We pushed

~~The~~ **the** door. It opened. The house was **dark and smelly** ~~smelly~~.

There were spiders everywhere. We ~~herd~~ **heard**

~~Sounds~~ **sounds** from the kitchen. What was it**?**

- Make the changes Dina's teacher made.
- Save the document again as **Dina's Work**.

Another story

- Here is another story.
- Copy the story exactly.
- Don't make any changes.
- Save the story as **crab1**.

Pinched by a crab

Last Saturday evening, I was bathing in the sea. Suddenly, something pinched one of my toes! I felt great pain and rushed out of the water.

I saw a crab on the toe. I shook off the crab from my toe and the pain went away.

My mum gave me a drink of juice and I felt much better.

Making changes

- Follow the marked story and make all the changes.
- Save the corrected story as **crab2**.

Pinched by a crab

Last ~~saturday~~ **Saturday** evening, I was bathing in the **river** ~~sea~~. Suddenly, something pinched one of my

toes**!** I felt great pain and rushed out of the

water.

I saw a crab on ~~the~~ **my** toe. I shook off the

crab from my ~~toe~~ **foot** and the pain went away.

My mum gave me a ~~drink of juice~~ **piece of fruit** and I felt much better.

Typing a story

➤ Type the story.

➤ Don't change anything. Don't tap ⏎Enter at the end of the line.

> Once when a huge Lion was asleep, a Mouse began up and down upon him him. This soon wakened the Lion. Rising up angrily, he caught him and wanted to kill him. The Mouse begged for forgiveness and promised to help the Lion one day! The Lion laughed and let him go.

➤ Save the story as Lion and Mouse.

Copy and paste

➤ Highlight the story.

➤ Click .

➤ Click the cursor at the end of the story.

➤ Tap ⏎Enter twice.

➤ Click .

➤ Save your story again.

You have just copied and pasted the story below the original story.

Edit the story

➤ Edit the story by making the following changes to the story you have just copied:

- o Deleting word:
  - Delete the word 'huge' from the phrase 'a huge Lion'
  - Delete the repeated word 'him'
- o Save your story.
- o Adding word:
  - Add the word 'little' between 'a' and 'Mouse' in the first sentence
  - Add the word 'running' between 'began' and 'up'
- o Save your story again.
- o Changing punctuation mark:
  - Change the full stop ' . ' after 'asleep' to a comma ' , '
  - Change the exclamation mark '!' after 'one day' to a full stop ' . '
- o Save your story again.

Spellchecker

➤ Use the spellchecker to make sure there are no other spelling mistakes.

➤ Type your name, class and school name at the bottom of the page.

➤ Click .

➤ Click Save As ▸.

➤ Save your edited copy as lion2.

Editing a story

- Open the file The Lion and The Mouse Part 2.docx.
- There are 9 errors in the passage.
- Proofread it carefully.
- Use the spellchecker to help you.
- Make sure it is error free.
- Save the passage with a new name.

Ask your teacher for the file if you cannot find it!

Edit the story

- Type the story with no changes.
- Do not tap ⏎ Enter .
- Save the story as Gifts.
- Use a pen to mark 8 mistakes in the story on the right.
- Use the spell-checker to correct the mistakes on the story file.
- Save the corrected story as Gifts2.

Gifts

Danny was walk home one find moring. He saw some pretty flowrs beside the path and piked them for his Mum. His mum was so please that she gave him a peece of cake to eat. Dan shared it with his sisster.

Printing

- Open the file Gifts2 that you have saved.
- Click 🖶 to print the file.

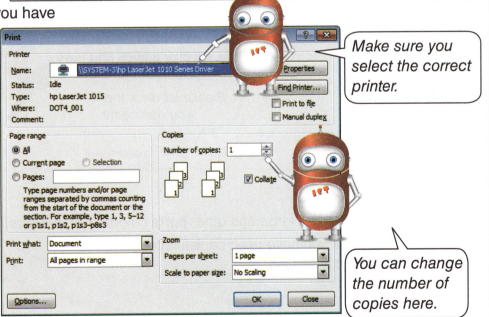

Make sure you select the correct printer.

You can change the number of copies here.

Optional extension and challenge activities

Module 1 – Starting with Text

Challenge 1 ›

Work with a friend.

- Type a rhyme you know.
- Cut and paste the lines into the wrong order.
- Ask your friend to put them into the correct order again.
- Save your work to your folder.

Challenge 2 ›

- Copy this invitation or write your own.

INVITATION

Please come to my party on

Wednesday 8 August 2012
from 5pm – 7pm

We will play games and have special food for tea.

Please let me know if you can come

- Make some text large and other parts coloured or in *italics*.
- Check that you have used capital letters and that it is correctly spelled.

Optional extension and challenge activities

Challenge 3

- Write a short story about a boy and his pet dragon.
- Save it as boystory.
- Select and change some words to make it a story about a girl with her pet cat.
- Save the story as girlstory.

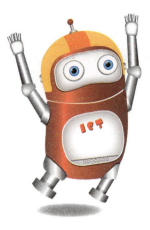

Module 2
Starting Images

Learning Objectives

	Student is able to:	Pass/Merit
1	Use simple shapes and lines to create pictures or patterns	P
2	Edit pictures, using visual effects	P
3	Add details to an existing picture, using straight lines or geometric shapes	P
4	Copy or delete character or object	M
5	Use 'save as' to store edited pictures	M

2.1 Paint

Start Paint

- Click 🪟 to open Start menu.
- Click ▶ **All Programs** .
- Click 📁 **Accessories** .
- Click 🎨 **Paint** .
- Listen carefully to your teacher's explanation.
- Write the following parts at the correct places.
  - ○ Paint button
  - ○ Tool box
  - ○ Drawing area
  - ○ Colour box
  - ○ Scroll bars

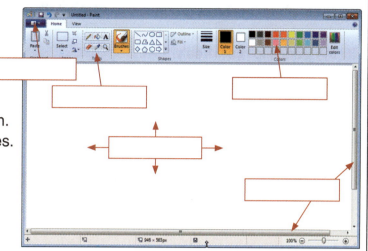

Tool box

- Place the mouse pointer on each tool icon.
- Do not click.
- Read each tool tip.
- Write the tool name in the correct box on the right.

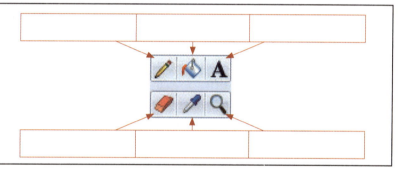

The Line tool ◣

- Click ◣ in the Shapes group.
- Choose the line thickness in ▤ Size .
- Place the mouse pointer at one point in the drawing area.
- Click the drawing area and holding the mouse button drag to a new position to make a new line.
- Release the mouse.
- Draw more lines of different colours and thickness.
- Holding the ⇧ *Shift* key while dragging the mouse will give you a perfect horizontal, vertical or diagonal straight line.

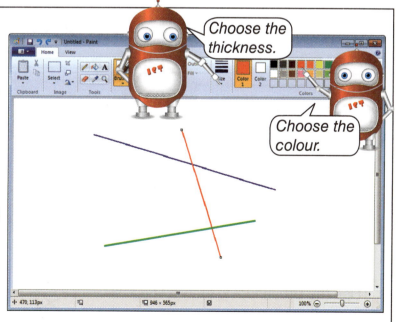

Choose the thickness.

Choose the colour.

The Pencil tool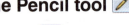

- Click in the Tools group.
- Click in the drawing area, drag the pencil to draw freely.

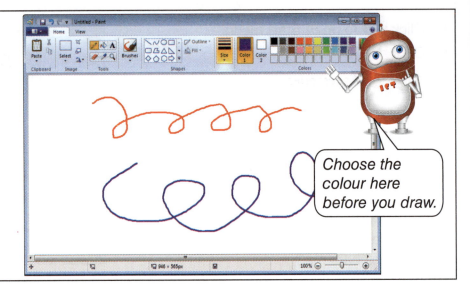

Choose the colour here before you draw.

The Brush tool

- Click Brushes.
- You can choose type of the brush before you draw.
- You can choose the brush size in Size.
- You can also choose the colour before you draw.

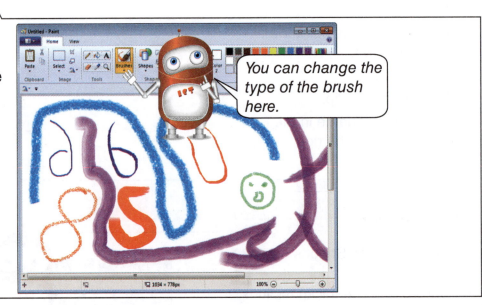

You can change the type of the brush here.

Make a line maze

- Click in the Shapes group.
- Change its thickness.
- Draw lines to make a maze.
- Click Brushes.
- Change the colour and shape of the Brush tool.
- Use the Brush tool to draw a line through your maze.

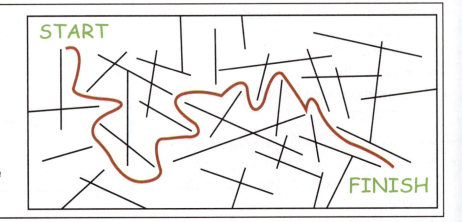

START

FINISH

The ellipse tool

- Click ⬭ in the Shapes group.
- Click and drag to draw a circle or an oval.

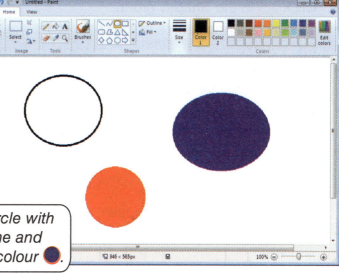

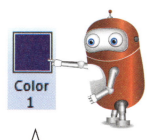

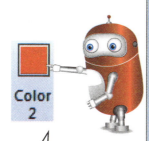

Select this to draw outline with the foreground colour ◯.

Select this to draw a circle with foreground colour outline and filled with background colour ⬤.

The Fill with colour tool

- Draw the outline.
- Click 🪣.
- Click in the circle to fill with the foreground colour selected.

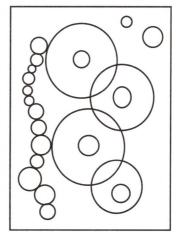

The Rectangle tool ▢

- Click ▢.
- Click and drag to draw a rectangle or square.
- Select from the options or use 🪣 to fill the rectangles with colours.

The Polygon tool

- Click in the Shapes group.
- To draw a triangle, click at the first vertex.
- Drag and click at the second vertex to draw the first line.
- Click at the third vertex to draw the second side.
- Click at the first vertex again to form the triangle.
- The type of triangle drawn depends on the fill style chosen.
- Draw the three triangles as shown.

Style 1 – foreground colour outline.

Style 2 – foreground colour outline; filled with background colour.

Style 3 – filled with foreground colour.

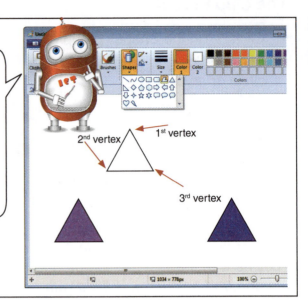

The Eraser tool

- If you make any mistake while drawing, you can erase the mistake and redraw the picture.
- Click in the Tools group.
- Place the eraser at the mistake and drag it across the mistake.

You can change the size of the eraser here.

Undo

- Draw a red circle.
- Draw a yellow rectangle inside the red circle.
- To remove the rectangle, click .

I just hold down Ctrl *and tap z!*

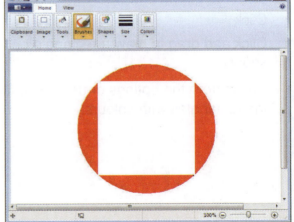

2.3 Duplicating images

Copy

- Draw a blue circle.

- Click 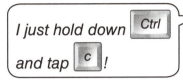 and click ⬚ **Rectangular selection**.

- Click and drag across the blue circle to select it.

- Click 🗐 **Copy**.

I just hold down `Ctrl` *and tap* `c` *!*

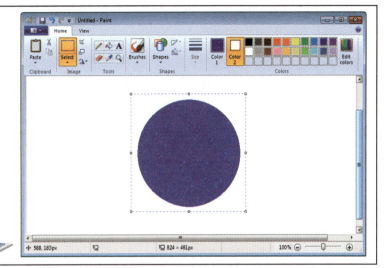

Paste

- Click .

- The duplicated image is placed at the top left corner.

I just hold down `Ctrl` *and tap* `v` *!*

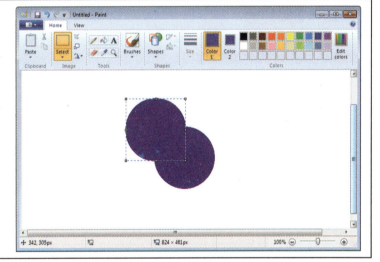

Move

- Use the mouse to drag the circle to a new place.

- Draw a red rectangle.

- Duplicate two more of it.

You can only move a shape when you can see the selection box around it.

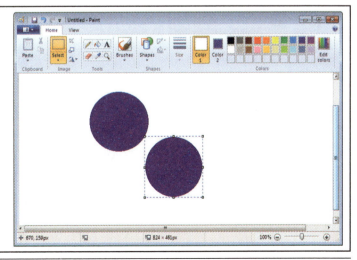

Traffic lights

- Draw a rectangle.
- Draw three small circles inside the rectangle.
- Draw two straight lines for the post.
- Fill in the appropriate colours yourself.

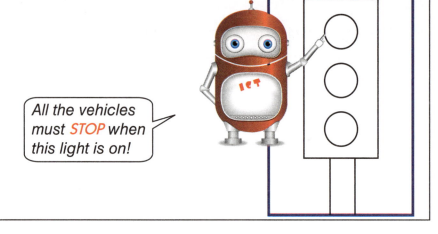

All the vehicles must STOP when this light is on!

Save as

- Click .
- Click **Save as**.
- Type a filename that you can remember easily.
- Start with your initials.

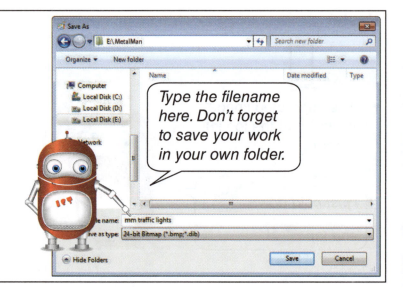

Type the filename here. Don't forget to save your work in your own folder.

Dragon

- Draw a small red square.
- Use **Rectangular selection** to select it.
- Copy and paste it.
- Drag it in front of the first square.
- Do this six times.
- Draw a circle for the face.
- Use a thick brush and new colours to add a new face, legs, wings and the tail.
- Save your picture as Dragon.

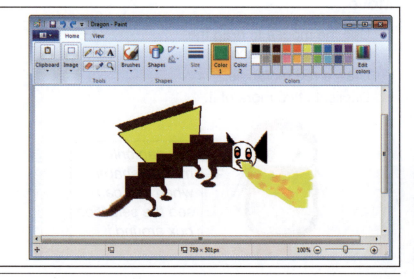

The curve tool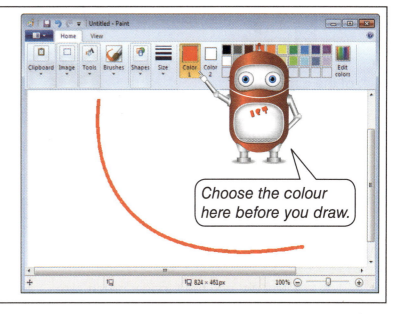

- Click ⟿ in the Shapes group.
- Draw a straight line.
- Click somewhere near the end of the line and drag to form the curve.
- Click somewhere near the other end of the line and drag to the same direction to form a smooth curve.

Choose the colour here before you draw.

Double curves

- Click ⟿ in the Shapes group.
- Draw a straight line.
- Click somewhere near the end of the line and drag to form the curve.
- Click somewhere near the other end of the line and drag to the opposite direction to form a double curve.

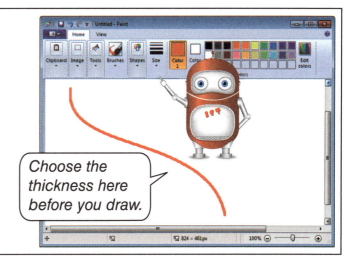

Choose the thickness here before you draw.

Coloured balls

- Draw 4 circles.
- Draw some curves to form the patterns.
- Fill with appropriate colours.
- Save your picture using a filename that you can remember easily.

*Remember: using **copy** and **paste** will save you time.*

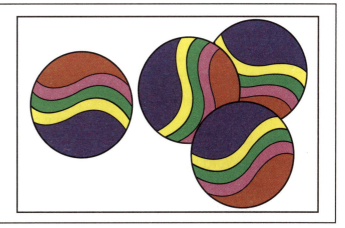

The air brush tool

- Click in Brushes.
- Try using the different sizes of the airbrush.

  Select the size of the airbrush here. Use the airbrush to write your name on the screen.

Choose the colour of the airbrush here.

Make a desert scene

- Click and choose the biggest brush size.
- Select dark blue.
- Spray the top of the sky.
- Change to a lighter blue and spray the sky lower down.
- Select yellow and spray the sand.
- Change the brush size to the smallest.
- Select blue and spray a pool.
- Save your picture with the filename desert.

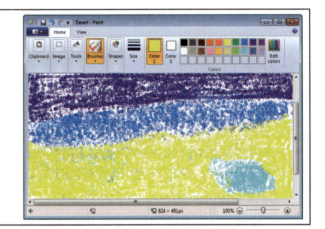

Word maze

- Click **A** in the Tools group.
- Drag a rectangular area on the drawing area.
- Click Text tab.
- Click Arial

  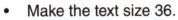

  Click here to choose the font.

- Make the text size 36.
- Type the word puzzle.
- Drag another rectangular area and type the word stop.
- Repeat to type other words: alley, road, turn, twist, touch, block, return and arrange the words around the screen to make a Word maze.
- Save the Word maze.
- Use or to draw a line through the Word maze.
- Save your Word maze with a different filename.

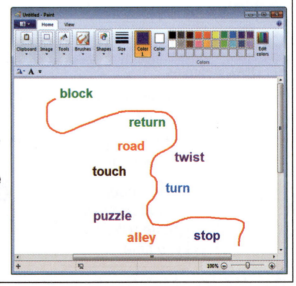

2.6 Editing pictures

More pictures

- Practise drawing more pictures using simple shapes, straight lines and brushes of different sizes.

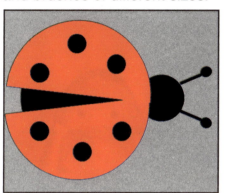

- Don't forget to save your pictures.

The snowman

- Use shapes, curves and lines to draw the snowman as shown.
- Save your picture as snowman.

Remember the filename of the picture and its location. You need this picture for the next exercise.

Making changes

- Open the file snowman that you have saved in the last exercise.
- Draw a tree near the snowman.
- Erase the rectangular eyes and redraw the eyes using circles.
- Erase the triangular nose and replace it with a long triangle.
- Erase the mouth and use the pencil or brush to draw a curve as the mouth.
- Add a red button between the two black buttons.
- Fill the background grey.
- Use the airbrush to add some snow.
- Save your edited picture as snowman2.

More pictures

- Draw the fish and the duck.
- Save the pictures for more exercises.

Modify the fish

- Open the picture fish.
- Remove the stone at the bottom left.
- Copy the small stone.
- Duplicate two more and place them next to it.
- Draw a line for the mouth.
- Add 4 bubbles.
- Add two lines for the fin.
- Add more leaves to the weed.
- Add a small white dot on the eye.
- Save the picture as fish2.

Modify the duck

- Open the picture duck.
- Change the colour of the bill to red.
- Use the brush to add three birds in the sky.
- Remove the fish.
- Duplicate the lily leaf and place it on the left side.
- Change the shape of the eye to a vertical oval shape.
- Add more leaves to the weeds.
- Fill the sky and water with two different colours of blue.
- Save the picture as duck2.

Optional extension and challenge activities

Module 2 – Starting Images

Challenge 1 ›

- Use drawing tools to make a pattern with shapes and lines. Fill some of the shapes with colour.
- Save the work as pattern1 and print it.
- Open the file and change the colour of 2 of the lines or shapes.
- Add 4 more small lines or shapes to the pattern.
- Save the work as pattern2 and print it.
- Challenge a friend to spot the 6 differences between the patterns.

Challenge 2 ›

- Use the ellipse tool to make a shape on the screen.
- Use the pencil tool to draw your name in the shape.
- Use the rectangle tool to draw a rectangle.
- Use the brush tool to draw your name in the rectangle.
- Change the colour and thickness of the brush and draw a pattern round your work.

Challenge 3

Make a firework picture.

- Use the polygon tool to draw a triangular firework case.
- Copy and paste the shape to make 3 triangles.
- Use the spray and line tools to add sparks.
- Use the eraser if you make a mistake.
- Save your work and make changes to it later.

Module 3
Starting Graphs

Learning Objectives

	Student is able to:	Pass/ Merit
1	Store and classify information	P
2	Present information in charts or graphs	P
3	Use charts or graphs to answer simple questions	P
4	Draw simple conclusions from charts or graphs	M

Simple data table

- Look at these coloured cars.
- Count the different colours.
- Write your answers in the table below.

red	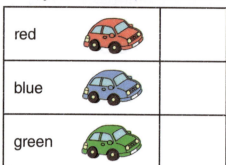	
blue		
green		

 Microsoft Office Excel 2007

- Open the program Excel.
- Click 📂 and open the Excel file colour_cars.xlsx provided.
- Complete the data table by filling in the number of each colour in column B.

Excel names the columns A, B, C, ... and names the rows 1, 2, 3, ...

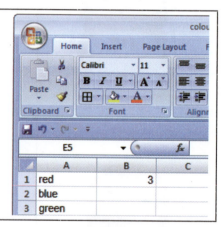

Make a pictogram

- Select and put the pictures of cars according to the colour and number in the 3x5 grid provided.
- You have just made a pictogram!
- Save your work as carsgraph.

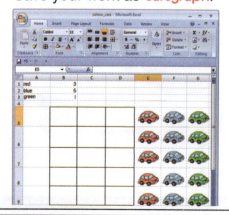

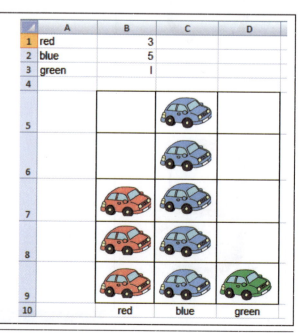

Pet graph

- Look at the pets on this page.
- Count the different kinds of pets.
- Open the Excel file pets.xlsx provided.
- Complete the data table.
- Type the names of the pets below the 4x4 grid: hamster, cat, rabbit, fish.
- Put the number of pictures according to the number in the data table.
- Save your work as petgraph.

	A	B	C	D	E	F	G	H	I	J
1	hamster	2								
2	cat									
3	rabbit									
4	fish									
5										
6										
7										
8										

Answering questions about the graph

- Look at the pet graph and answer the following questions.

1. Which is the most popular pet?

   _____

2. Which is the least popular pet?

   _____

3. Which are more popular, fish or hamsters?

   _____

4. Which is less popular, the cat or the fish?

   _____

Favourite fruit

- The following is the survey of the favourite fruit of 20 children.

Melon	6
Pineapple	2
Banana	4
Grape	3
Orange	5

- Open the Excel file fav_fruit.xlsx
- Complete the data table.
- Use the graphics and the grid provided to draw a pictogram.
- Save your work using a new filename.

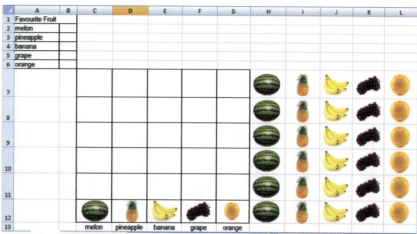

- Answer the following questions:

1. How many children like the pineapple?

_____

2. Which is the most popular fruit?

_____

3. Which is the least popular fruit?

_____

4. Which fruit is more popular, melon or orange?

_____

Preparing for a different chart

- There are other ways of presenting the data.
- Open the worksheet fav_fruit2.xlsx
- Refer to the previous exercise and complete the data table.

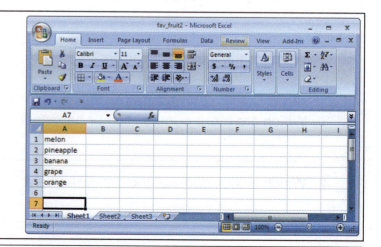

Make a Chart

- Highlight the data table.

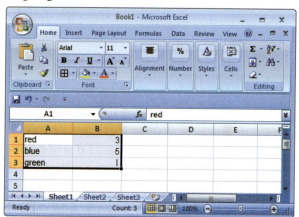

- Click on Insert tab.

- Click .

- In 2-D column, click .

Title and axes

- Select the chart.

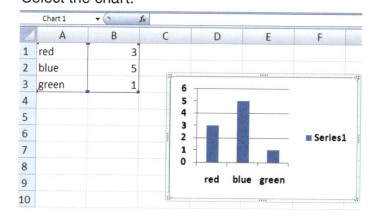

- Click on Layout tab.

- Click to set the position of the data.

- Click to set the title.

- Click to label the axes.

Legend

- The legend tells you more about the data if you use column headings.

- To delete a legend click on Layout tab.

- Click Legend and click Turn off Legend.

You do not need to show any legend for a simple column chart.

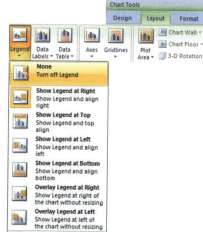

Chart location

- The finished graph can be placed in the same worksheet, together with the data table.
- You can make some adjustment to the location and size of the graph.

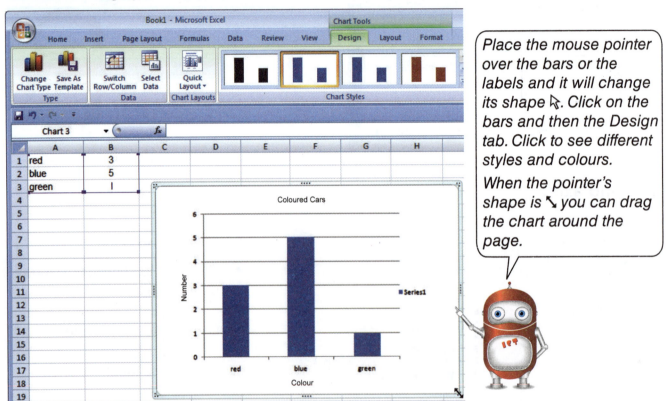

Place the mouse pointer over the bars or the labels and it will change its shape ☝. Click on the bars and then the Design tab. Click to see different styles and colours.

When the pointer's shape is ↖ you can drag the chart around the page.

Resize the graph

- You may need to resize the graph.
- Click the chart to see ↖.
- Put the pointer over one corner of the chart to see ↖ placeholder.
- Click and drag to resize the chart.
- Try this with each place holder in turn.

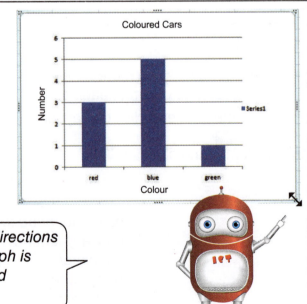

Dragging in diagonal directions will ensure that the graph is increased or decreased proportionately.

Selecting one column

- Click somewhere in the first column.
- Dots around all the three columns indicate they are all selected.

- Click in the first column again.
- Only the first column is selected now.

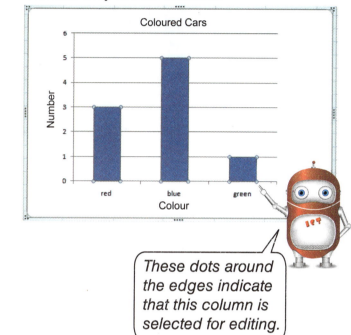

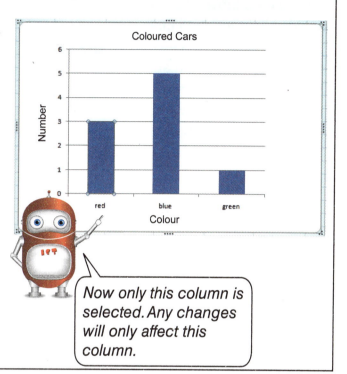

These dots around the edges indicate that this column is selected for editing.

Now only this column is selected. Any changes will only affect this column.

Changing column colour

- With one column selected, click on Home tab and choose 🪣 .
- Select a colour for the column.
- Make each column a different colour.
- Save your work.

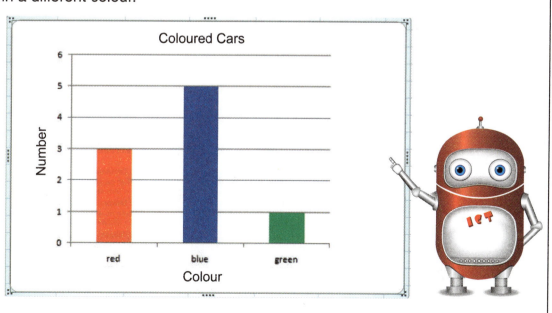

3-D column chart

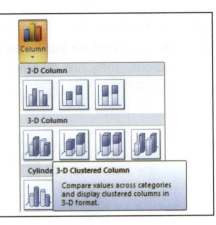

- Open the worksheet pets2.xlsx.
- Refer to the previous exercise and complete the data table.
- Highlight the data table.

- Click on Insert tab and click Column.
- Choose Column for Chart type.
- Choose 3-D Clustered column for chart sub-type.
- Click Series label and backspace to delete the legend.

3-D pet chart

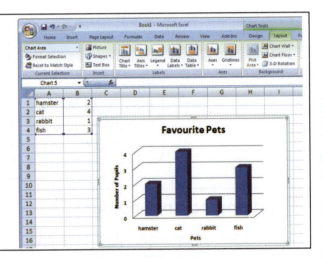

- Complete the chart:
  - Type Favourite Pets as the chart title.
  - Type Pets as the Category (X) axis.
  - Type Number of Pupils as the Value (Y) axis.
- Don't forget to delete the legend.
- Place the final graph in the same worksheet.
- Adjust the size and position of the graph.
- Save the worksheet.

Refining the chart

- If your chart shows decimals we must change this.
- Select the chart and click the Layout tab.

- Click Axes and then

  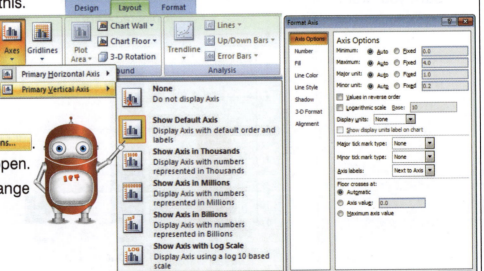

  Primary Vertical Axis ▸.
- Click More Primary Vertical Axis Options...
- The Format Axes box will open.
- Click on Axis Options and change both the Major Unit and Minor unit to 1.
- Click Close.

Changing alignment

- You can change the way the axis labels are shown.
- Click on an axis label.

- On Home tab, click on 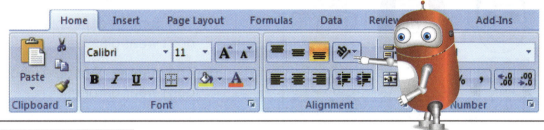 in the Alignment group.
- Click to see the text vertical or at an angle.

Final graph

- Based on the graph drawn, answer the following questions:
1. Which pet is more popular, the rabbit or the hamster?

_____

2. Which is less popular, the hamster or the fish?

_____

3. Among hamster, rabbit and fish, which is the most popular pet?

_____

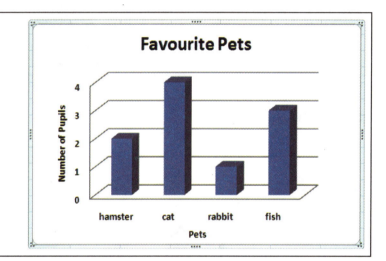

Minibeasts

- Look at the picture of minibeasts.
- Use Excel to set up a data table.
- Use these categories: snails, slugs, insects, spiders, and milipedes.
- Draw a 3-D column graph on these minibeasts.
- Answer the following questions:
1. How many millipedes are there?

_____

2. Which is more, spiders or insects?

_____

3. Which minibeasts are there twice as many of as slugs?

_____

Insects have six legs.

Group people

- Look at these faces.

- Draw column charts to show:

  o The number of people who wear / don't wear hats.

  o The number of people who wear / don't wear glasses.

  o The number of people who wear / don't wear earrings.

  o The number of people who are / aren't smiling.

- Write 1 observation about each of the charts.

Favourite flowers

- The picture above shows the favourite flowers of 15 girls.
- Open the file flowers.xlsx.
- Count the number of each flower and fill in the data table.
- Draw a 3-D column chart based on the data table.
- Label your 3-D chart:
  o Chart title: Favourite flowers
  o Category (X) axis: Flowers
  o Value (Z) axis: Number of girls
- Based on the chart, answer questions 1 and 2.
1. How many girls favour hibiscus?

   _____

2. Write down 2 sensible but simple general statements about the graph on favourite flowers that you have drawn.

   a. _____

   b. _____

Interhouse Sports Meet

- The following shows the result of the 2013 interhouse sports meet of a certain school.
  - o Red House: 2 Gold medals
  - o Blue House: 4 Gold medals
  - o Green House: 5 Gold medals
  - o White House: 3 Gold medals
  - o Orange House: 6 Gold medals
- Open the file sports2013.xlsx and complete the data table provided.
- Use the pictures provided to produce a pictogram.
- Based on the pictogram,
  - o Which house is the Champion of the Sports meet for 2013?

    _____

  - o Which houses have done better than the White House?

    _____

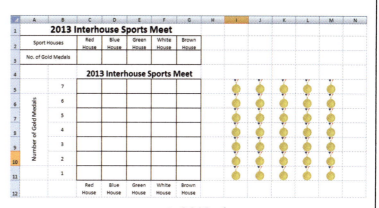

sports2013.xlsx

Click and drag the number of medals into the columns based on the data table. NOT all the pictures will be used.

Examination results

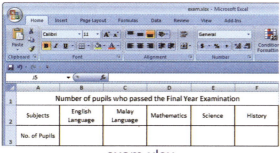

Subjects	English Language	Malay Language	Mathematics	Science	History
No. of Pupils					

Number of pupils who passed the Final Year Examination

exam.xlsx

- The data below shows the number of pupils who failed the final year examination results.
  - o English Language: 5 pupils
  - o Malay Language: 2 pupils
  - o Mathematics: 6 pupils
  - o Science: 4 pupils
  - o History: 2 pupils
- Open the file exam.xlsx.
- Draw a column or a bar chart based on the data table.

- Label your chart:
  - o Chart title: Number of pupils who failed the final year examination
  - o Category (X) axis: Subjects
  - o Value (Y) axis: Number of pupils
- Based on the chart drawn,
  - o Which subjects have more than 4 failures?

    _____

  - o How many pupils failed Science?

    _____

- Deduce 2 simple but sensible general statements about the chart.

  a. _____

  b. _____

Optional extension and challenge activities

Module 3 – Starting Graphs

Challenge 1

- Use the pictures from the file pets.xlsx to make a pictogram to show the pets your friends would like to have if they could each have a new one.
- Use the chart to see what is the most wanted pet, and if people would prefer cats or rabbits.

Challenge 2

- Find out about the colours of the bikes your friends have or would like to have.
- Make a bar chart to show what are the most popular colours for bikes.

Challenge 3

- Test your friends to see who can do the most skips with a rope without stopping or who can bounce a ball the most times without losing it.
- Make a chart to show your results.
- Are boys better than girls at either task?

Module 4
Starting Control

Learning Objectives

	Student is able to:	Pass/Merit
1	Give a screen turtle a set of instructions to achieve a specified objective	P
2	Record the instructions to the turtle	P
3	Use angles other than 90 or 180 degrees	M
4	Create a set of instructions involving at least five moves to achieve a specific target	M

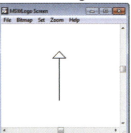
Forward (fd)

- Click at the bottom of the commander.
- Type forward 100. There must be a space between forward and 100.
- Tap ⟵ Enter.
- The screen turtle moves forward 100 units, leaving a line of 100 units long.

To start MSWLogo double-click 🖊 from your desktop. Ask your teacher if you can't find it. Click here to start typing commands.

This is called the screen turtle.

Home, clean

- Click at the bottom of the commander.
- Type home and tap ⟵ Enter. The screen turtle returns to the start position. The line stays.
- Type clean and tap ⟵ Enter. The line disappears.
- Type home clean and tap ⟵ Enter. The turtle returns home without leaving any line.

Equivalent moves

- Type fd 50 and tap ⟵ Enter.
- The turtle moves forward and draws a line of 50 units.
- Type fd 30 and tap ⟵ Enter. The turtle continues to move forward and draws a line of 30 units.
- Type home clean and tap ⟵ Enter.
- Type fd 80 and tap ⟵ Enter.

The effect of fd 80 is the same as fd 50 followed by fd 30.

Equivalent commands

- Type home clean and tap ⟵ Enter.
- Type fd 30 fd 50 and tap ⟵ Enter. The effect of fd 30 fd 50 is the same as fd 80.
- What is the single command that gives the same effect as fd 20 fd 40 fd 70?

When you type compound commands like fd 30 fd 50, you only leave a space between the commands and the step (figure). DO NOT type any comma, it is not a MSWLogo command.

Back (bk)

- Type **home clean** and tap ⏎Enter .
- Type **fd 120** and tap ⏎Enter .
- Type **bk 120** and tap ⏎Enter .
- Where is the position of the turtle now?

_____

- Type **home clean** and tap ⏎Enter .
- Type **fd 150** and tap ⏎Enter .
- Type **bk 80 bk 70** and tap ⏎Enter .
- Type **fd 100 bk 10** and tap ⏎Enter .

> *Back* or *bk* will cause the turtle to move backwards, just opposite to *Forward* or *fd*.
> Similarly, the combination of *bk 80 bk 70* is the same as *bk 150*.
> The command *fd 100 bk 100* will cause the turtle to draw a line of 100 units and then go back to the original position.

PenPaint (PPT), PenErase (PE)

- Type **home clean** and tap ⏎Enter .
- Type **fd 150** and tap ⏎Enter .
- Type **pe** and tap ⏎Enter .
- Type **bk 150** and tap ⏎Enter .

> *After the command pe (penerase), the turtle will erase its path either fd or bk. Use this to erase mistakes. Before you redraw, you must give the command ppt (pen paint).*

- Type **fd 100** and tap ⏎Enter .
- The turtle only moves forward without drawing any line.
- Type **ppt** and tap ⏎Enter .
- Type **fd 50** and tap ⏎Enter .
- The turtle is back to normal.
- Type **home clean** and tap ⏎Enter .
- Type **fd 200** and tap ⏎Enter .
- Type **pe bk 200** and tap ⏎Enter .
- Type **ppt fd 180** and tap ⏎Enter .

Right half turn

- Type **right 90** or **rt 90**.
- Right or rt orders the turtle to turn to the right.
- Right 90 or rt 90 orders the turtle to make a quarter turn to the right.
- Type **rt 180**.
- rt 180 will order the turtle to do a half turn.

> *A quarter turn means a 90° turn. However, we do not type the symbol for degree (°).*

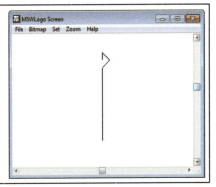

Left turn (lt)

- Type left 90 or lt 90.
- Left or lt orders the turtle to turn the left.
- Left 90 or lt 90 orders the turtle to make a quarter turn to the left.
- Type lt 180.
- lt 180 orders the turtle to do a half turn.
- Type the following commands, tapping ⏎ Enter after typing each line.

  fd 150 rt 90
  fd 200 rt 90
  fd 150 rt 90
  fd 200

- Name the geometrical shape formed.

  _____

- Type the following commands, tapping after typing each line.

  fd 200 rt 90
  fd 300 rt 90
  fd 300 rt 90
  fd 600 rt 180
  fd 200 lt 90
  fd 200 lt 90
  fd 150 rt 180
  fd 300

- Tap PrtSc to capture your work. Open MS Word and click 📋 to paste the image into the blank document. Print a copy and glue the copy in the space below.

Your print out

Glue your printed copy here.

4.2 More commands

Pen Up (PU), Pen Down (PD)

- Type **pu fd 100** and tap .
- Pen up! The turtle will move forward 100 units without drawing any line.
- Type **pd rt 90 fd 100** and tap ⏎Enter.
- Pen down! The turtle will again draw the line.
- Type **home clean** and tap ⏎Enter.
- Type the following commands and tap ⏎Enter. after each line.

  fd 200 rt 90
  pu fd 100 rt 90
  fd 100 rt 90
  pd fd 200

- What object was just drawn by the above commands? _____

I don't know how to...
This is how the turtle will respond to you if you do not give the relevant MSWLogo commands. Because it does not know what or how to execute the commands!

Changing pen colour

- Click **Set**.
- Click **PenColor...**.
- Select the red colour and click .
- Type the following commands:

  fd 150 rt 90. Tap ⏎Enter.

- Repeat the commands another three times.
- Do you get a red square?

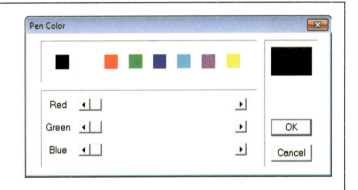

Changing pen size

- Click **Set**.
- Click **Pen Size...**.
- Click ▬ and click **OK**.
- Type the following commands:

  fd 100 lt 90. Tap ⏎Enter.

- Repeat the commands another three times.
- Do you get a square with thicker outline?

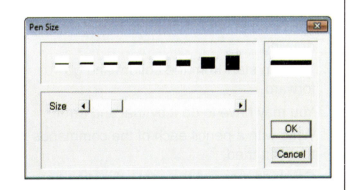

Other angles

- Change your pen colour to red.
- Type the following commands. Remember to tap ⏎Enter after each line.

fd 10 rt 60
fd 20 rt 60
fd 30 rt 60
fd 40 rt 60
fd 50 rt 60
fd 60 rt 60

- Continue the commands until fd 150.
- Repeat for different colours and different angles (e.g. 30, 45, 120, 135).

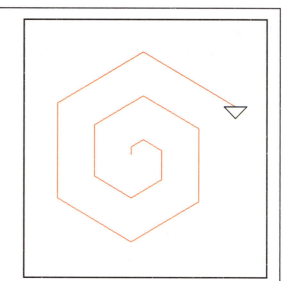

Drawing letters

- Set the pen colour to red.
- Set the pen size to ▬ .
- Type the following commands:

fd 200
rt 135 fd 150
lt 90 fd 150
rt 135 fd 200

- Click Bitmap .
- Click SaveAs... .
- Type letterM and click Save .

Trial and error

- Draw the letter Y and write down all the commands below.
- You need at least 4 steps to complete the drawing.
- You can start from the bottom and go forward.
- You may have to do it by trial and error.
- Write with a pencil each of the commands that you tried.
- Combine steps of the same direction and rewrite the commands.

- E.g. combine fd 30 fd 50 into fd 80.

_____

_____

_____

_____

_____

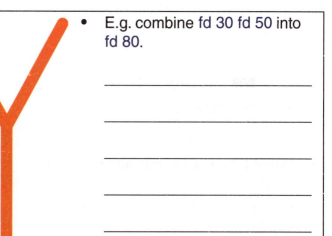

Letter E

- First write on a piece of paper what are the steps that you would take to draw the letter E.
- Type the commands to try it out.
- Refine the commands and write them below:

_____

_____

_____

_____

_____

_____

You do not have to draw an E exactly like the one shown here!

Letter K

- First write on a piece of paper what are the steps that you would take to draw the letter K.
- Type the commands to try it out.
- Refine the commands and write them below:

_____

_____

_____

_____

You only need to draw a letter K similar to the one shown here!

Letter X

- First write on a piece of paper what are the steps that you would take to draw the letter X.
- Type the commands to try it out.
- Refine the commands and write them below:

_____

_____

_____

_____

You can try 60° for the smaller angle.

Treasure hunt

- Click Bitmap .

- Click Load... .

- Look for the file collect7diamonds.bmp.

- Your mission is to collect all the seven diamonds.

- You must follow the exact sequence to collect the diamonds from diamond 1 to diamond 7.

- You are advised to write each command that you would use on a piece of paper and try it out.

- In your trial you may use more than 1 command.

- If you make mistakes that cannot be changed, you can always re-load the bitmap file given.

- When you have completed the treasure hunt, rearrange and refine or simplify the commands.

- Write down the commands you used for getting each diamond.

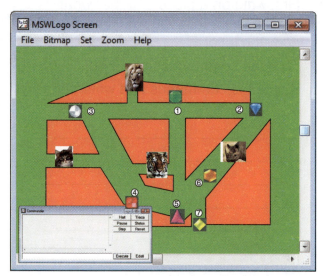

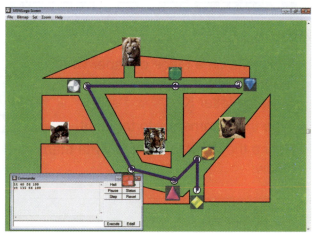

1. _____

2. _____

3. _____

4. _____

5. _____

6. _____

7. _____

- After writing down all the commands, click Bitmap , click Load... to load the same bitmap file again. Do not save changes to the bitmap file.

- Re-enter all commands until you have collected all the seven diamonds, then tap PrtSc to get a screen grab of the routes.

- Open MS Word and click to paste the screen grab.

- Save the document as diamonds.

- Print a copy and glue the printed copy on the next page.

When writing the commands, combine similar commands into a single command. e.g. *rt 30 rt 15 fd 100 fd 150 fd 100 can be written as rt 45 fd 350.*

Evidence of work done

Print the file *diamonds.docx* from the previous exercise. Glue it on this page (you are allowed to cover me!) as evidence of the work done.

Optional extension and challenge activities

Module 4 – Starting Control

Challenge 1

- Use a screen turtle to draw some digital numbers. Make the numbers different colours and thicknesses.

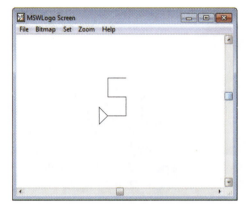

Challenge 2

- Plan how you will use the turtle to draw two triangles on the screen that are not joined by a line.
- Use a thick pen to draw a single line round each without touching them.

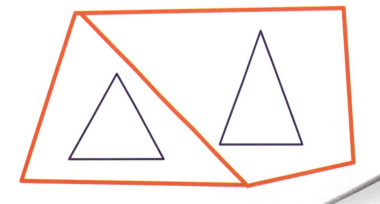

Challenge 3

- Use the turtle to draw some shapes on the screen to make a maze.
- Draw a thick line through your maze from the top right of the screen to the bottom left.

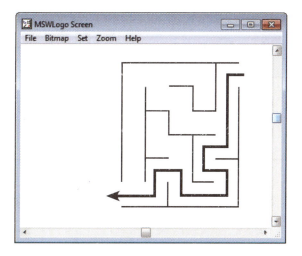

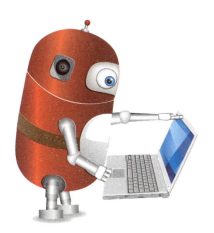

Module 5
Starting Searches

Learning Objectives

	Student is able to:	Pass/ Merit
1	Use buttons, menus and indexes to search for and navigate to information	P
2	Use keywords to search for information	P
3	Provide evidence of research undertaken	P
4	Select appropriate keywords	M
5	Select appropriate results	M

5.1 Using buttons and hotspots

Australia

- How much do you know about other countries like Australia, the USA, etc.? Use the name of the country as a keyword to find out.
- Use your browser to find Google.
- Type the word Australia in the Google search box.
- Click .
- Open the Wikipedia page.
- Find out the following information:
  - o   What is the capital of Australia?

    _____

  - o   What is the population of Australia?

    _____

  - o   What is the Australian currency?

    _____

- Tap  key and ↓ key to see all the pictures.
- Click on the relevant image.
- Click ← button to go back to the previous page.
- Type Koala into the Google search box.
- Choose a page such as Kids National Geographic.
- Find out three facts about Koala and write them here.

_____

_____

_____

_____

> When you point at some images the arrow turns to a hand to show a link to more information.

USA

- Type USA in the Google search box.
- Click .
- What is the full name of the USA?

  _____

- Add the word anthem to the search box.
- Open YouTube and listen to the National anthem of the USA.
- Use Google to find and listen to the National anthem of another country.

5.2 Index and hyperlink

Index

- Type Natural History Museum into the Google search box.
- Where is the Natural History Museum?

  _____

- When was it opened?

  _____

- Move the mouse over the index for the museum on the Google page to see the pointer change to a hand. This shows where there are links to other sections.
- Write the names of the six sections shown in the index here.

  _____   _____   _____

  _____   _____   _____

Hyperlink

- On the Google page, click the Kids only link for the Natural History Museum. This is a hyperlink.
- Follow the hyperlink to the Dinosaur page.
- Move the mouse over the page to see hyperlinks to other pages.
- Follow a link which interests you to find three facts about dinosaurs.
- Write them here.

_____

_____

_____

_____

_____

_____

_____

Birds

- Type Bird in the Google search box.
- Scroll up and down the page with the scroll bars to see how many entries there are on the page.
- Click the Images hyperlink at the top of the page and list the names of three birds.

  _____

  _____

  _____

- On the Google search page, type bird hatching. Follow a hyperlink to see a bird hatch.
- On the Google search page, type bird calls. Follow a hyperlink to hear some bird calls.

Penguins

- Type Penguin into the Google search box.
- See how many entries you get which do not seem to be about birds.
- Type Penguin + bird into the Google search box.
- Follow a link to a site about penguins.
- Follow the Penguins link to http://www.kidcyber.com.au/topics/penguin.htm.
- Complete the following passage.

Penguins are _____which cannot fly. They are good at _____ in the water. Penguins live in _____. They find _____in the sea. They nest on

_____.

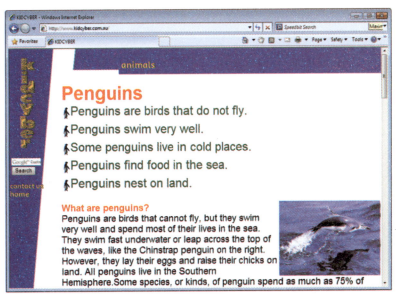

Keyword

- Type ants, not ant into the Google search box. Ants is your keyword.
- Type ants + leaf into the Google search box. Two keywords will give different results.
- Type ants + lift into the Google search box. These keywords will give new results.
- Follow a link to find out 3 facts about how much ants can lift.

Evidence of search

Tap PrtSc to grab a screen showing an ant lifting something. Open a new blank page in MS Word. Click to paste the image. Save it as ant.

Print a hard copy of the page and glue it on this page.

5.5 Finding information

Identifying a keyword

> *Most lions live in Africa or Asia. They live in groups called prides. They hunt together to catch zebra and other large mammals. The male lions are larger than the females and have a shaggy mane around their necks. Most hunting is done by the female lions who work together to ambush their prey.*

- Read the passage above. List the keywords you would use to find the answers to the following questions.

  1. Where do most lions live?

     _____

  2. What is a group of lions called?

     _____

  3. What do lions hunt?

     _____

  4. How do lions hunt?

     _____

- Use Google images to find a picture of lions hunting. Do a screen grab of a picture.

- Paste the image into a new MS Word document.

- Save the document with a suitable file name.

- Do the same with a second image.

Do it yourself

List the keywords you would use to find the answers to the following questions.

1. What do spiders make their webs from?

   _____

- Write down the keywords you used to find the answer to this question.

  _____

2. How do snakes kill their prey?

   _____

- Write down the keywords you used to find the answer to this question.

  _____

3. How high can a frog jump?

   _____

- Write down the keywords you used to find the answer to this question.

  _____

Evidence of search

Print the files containing your screen grab from the previous exercise. Glue them on this page (you are allowed to cover me!) as evidence of successful searches.

Optional extension and challenge activities

Module 5 – Starting Searches

Challenge 1

- Use keywords in a search engine such as Google to find out about your country.
- Copy a map of the country to a MS Word document and save it.
- See if you can find a recording of your national anthem to hear.
- Find out about fun things to do with kids in your country.

Challenge 2

- Make a fact file for kids about a rainforest or national park such as Taman Negara.
- Find out about the animals and plants that live there.
- Copy pictures to illustrate your file.
- Write the facts in your own words.

Challenge 3

- Use key words in a search engine to find out about an animal you like.
- Use the information to make a poster about it.

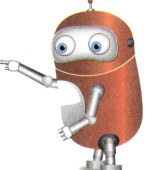

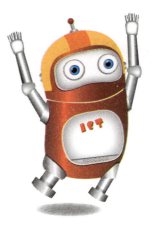

Module 6
Starting Email

Learning Objectives

	Student is able to:	Pass/ Merit
1	Collect and read email messages	P
2	Reply to email messages	P
3	Create and send email messages	P
4	Use email folders	M
5	Forward email messages and copy to another recipient	M

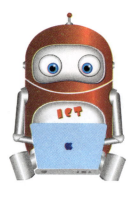

6.1 Email account

Setting up an account

- Your teacher will help you to set up your account.

- Most email addresses are simple, e.g. someone@somewhere.com

- Write your email address below. Learn and remember it.

  _____

- Most end with a country name.

  o .uk means United Kingdom

  o .hk means Hong Kong

  o .au means Australia

  o .cn means China

  o .in means India

  o .my means Malaysia

  o .sg means Singapore

Learn a friend's email address

- Write down a friend's email address so you can send him or her messages.

  _____

Write down the address exactly. There aren't usually any spaces in an email address.

Receiving and opening email

- Open [icon] Microsoft Office Outlook 2007 .

- Click [icon] **Inbox** to see the messages you have been sent.

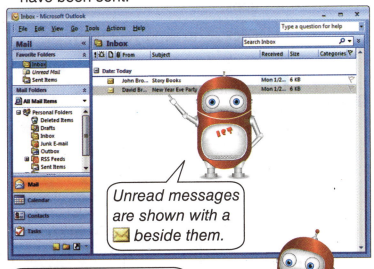

Unread messages are shown with a ✉ beside them.

You can see whom the message is from, and what it is about in the subject box.

- Double-click on the first message to open it.

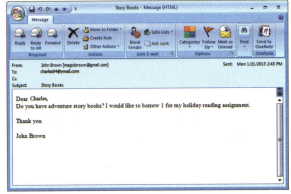

- Read the message and fill in the following:

  From:

  _____

  Date:

  _____

  To: _____

  Subject:

  _____

Replying to email

- Click 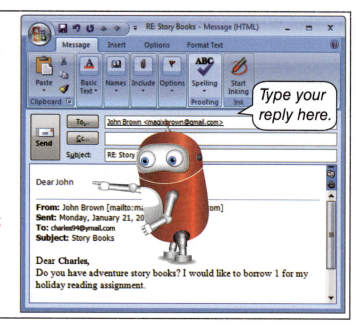.
- ![Microsoft Office Outlook 2007] will fill in the `To...` box automatically with the sender's name.
- ![Microsoft Office Outlook 2007] also fills in the `Subject:` box with Re: + the original subject.
- Click the space on top of the original message and type the reply:

Dear John,

Yes, my daddy has bought me some adventure storybooks. You can come to my house and select any of the books that you like.

Regards,
Charles

- Click ![Send] to send your reply.

New Year's Eve party

- Double-click on the second email from David Brown.

- Read the email message and fill in the following:

From: _____

Date: _____

To: _____

Subject: _____

- Click ![Reply].

- Reply to the email. Tell David that you are going to attend his New Year's Eve party.

Dear David,

Thank you very much for inviting me to your New Year's Eve party. I am glad to inform you that I will definitely attend and celebrate this great occasion with you!

Happy New Year!

Charles

- Tap `PrtSc` to do a screen grab of your reply.

- Paste the image in a new MS Word document and save it as reply.

- Print a hard copy of the document and glue it on the last page of this book.

- Click ![Send] to send your reply.

Ask your teacher how to have the two emails sent to your inbox.

You can type your own name instead of Charles'.

Creating a new message

- Write an email message to say thank you to David.

- Click  .

- Type the email address of David in the To... box: brwn_dvd@yahoo.com

- Type Thank you in the box.

- Type the following text:

Dear David,

I write to thank you for the wonderful time I had at your house last weekend. Both you and your family were very kind to me. I shall not forget the exciting visit to the National Zoo. I liked the lovely penguins very much. I also enjoyed the picnic we had in the National Park waterfall. The weekend was one of the best I have ever spent.

Once again, thank you for your family's kindness.

Regards,

Charles

Sending the message

- Read through the email that you have just composed to make sure that there are no spelling errors.

- Tap PrtSc to get a screen grab of your email.

- Paste the image in a new MS Word document and save it as newmail.

- Print a hard copy and glue it in the empty space below.

- Click to send out the email.

Glue your hard copy here.

Drafts folder

- Click  .
- Type richard_pqr@hotmail.com in the `To...` box.

> *You can type the email address of your own friend.*

- Type Congratulations in the `Subject:` box.
- Type the following text:

Dear Richard,

I am glad to learn that you have passed the recent UPSR examination with flying colours.

- Click .
- Click `Save` .
- Your message is saved in your 'Drafts' folder.

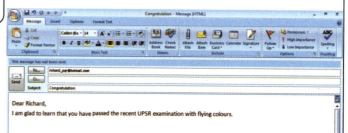

Edit a saved copy

- Click `Drafts` .
- Double-click the subject 'Congratulations' to open the saved draft.
- Complete the message:

A hard-working pupil like you deserve all the A grades. My parents too are glad of your success. Congratulations!

Keep up the good work. I am proud to be your friend.

Charles

- Click `Send` to send your message.

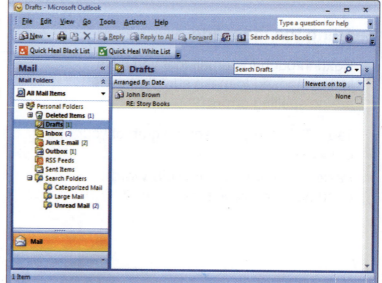

Outbox

- Click `Outbox` .
- If you have not connected to the Internet, the emails that you have sent by clicking `Send` will be stored in this folder.
- Double-click on any of the messages stored here to open it for editing.

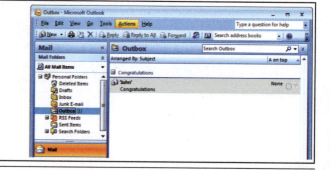

Sent items

- Click  Sent Items.
- Copies of the email messages that you have sent out will be stored in this folder.
- You cannot edit the stored messages in this folder.
- Select a message that you do not wish to keep, click ✗ to delete the message.

Click here to delete the sent message.

Deleted items

- Click 🗑 Deleted Items.
- This folder is the recycle bin.
- All the messages that you have deleted are stored here.
- If you have deleted the message accidentally, you can recover it.
- Select the message that you want to recover.
- Click Edit.
- Click Copy to Folder....
- Select the folder where you wish to place the recovered message.
- The selected message will remain in the deleted item folder.

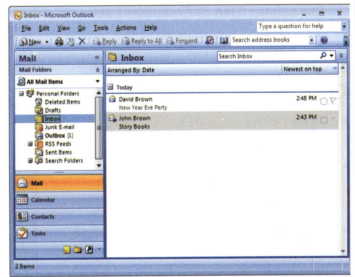

- Select the folder where you wish to place the recovered message.
- The selected message will be moved to the selected folder.
- If you are sure you do not wish to keep the message any longer, you can delete it permanently.
- Select the message to be removed.
- Click ✗.

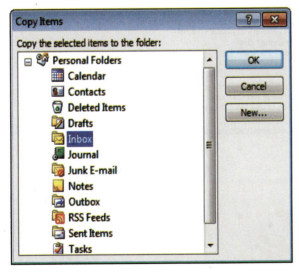

- You can also click on  Move to Folder....

Forward a message

- You are the chairman of the school computer club.
- You have received a request to use the computer lab.
- You do not have the authority to decide and you wish to refer to the teacher-in-charge of the computer lab.
- Open 📧 **Inbox** .
- Double-click on the message with the subject 'Use of Computer Lab'.
- Click 📧 **Forward** .

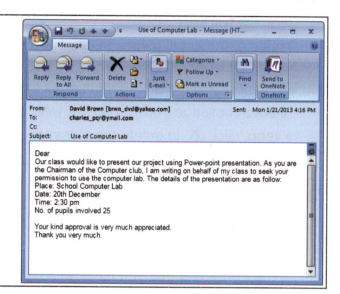

Copy to (Cc)

- Type fatimah@dares.com.my in the **To...** box.
- Type the email address of the sender of the email, David Brown, brwn_dvd@yahoo.com in the **Cc...** box.
- This will send a copy of the message back to him so that he knows the action you have taken.
- Microsoft Office Outlook has filled in the subject with Fw: before following it with the original subject.
- Click at the empty space on top of the original message and type the message:

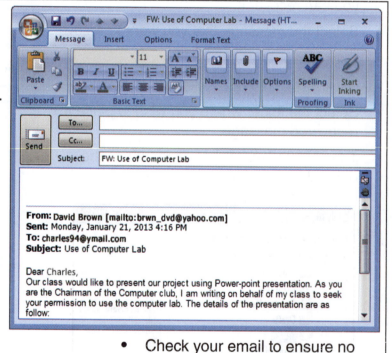

Dear Madam Fatimah,

I am forwarding an email from my friend, David Brown, to you. He would like to make use of the computer lab on 20th December to do a PowerPoint presentation. Please advise me whether permission can be granted. The details of the presentation are in the email forwarded.

For your information, we do not have any activity during that period of time.

Thank you and regards,

Charles

- Check your email to ensure no typing errors before you send it out.
- Click 📧 **Send** to send.

Mdm Fatimah's

- Click 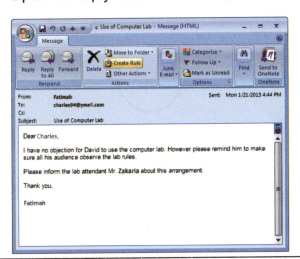 Inbox.
- Make sure you have the unread reply from the teacher, Mdm Fatimah.
- Do a screen grab of the Inbox to show the unread reply.
- Paste the captured image in a new MS Word document.
- Save it as ReplyFrom Teacher.
- Open the reply from the teacher, Mdm Fatimah.

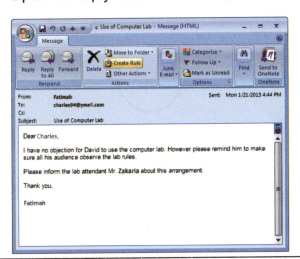

- Forward the email to David to inform him, with the text:

Dear David,

I am pleased to inform you that Mdm Fatimah has granted Permission for you to use the computer lab on 20th Dec. 2013 at 2.00 p.m.

Please remind your audience that all the rules of the lab must be observed.

Our lab attendant, Mr.Zakaria, will be around to open and close the lab for you.

Regards,

Charles

Cc

- Send a copy to the attendant Mr. Zakaria, using the address zakaria88@yahoo.com
- Do another screen grab of the email prepared by you and place it below the first screen grab.
- Save it again.
- You were happy about the condition of the computer lab after David used it for the presentation.
- Write a report to your teacher, Mdm Fatimah. Tell her that everything was in good order.
- Send a copy of your report to David too.
- Do a screen grab of your report.
- Place it in a new MS Word document.
- Save it with a suitable name and record the filename here: _____

Ask your teacher about the reply from Mdm Fatimah if you cannot find it in your Inbox.

Optional extension and challenge activities

Module 6 – Starting email

Challenge 1

- Send an email to your teacher telling her about the lessons which you enjoy the most.

Challenge 2

- Write an email story with a friend.
- You should each write one or two sentences and then click send.
- Read what your friend has added to the tale before you write the next part.

Challenge 3

- Send an email to a company to ask about one of its products.
- You could choose a sweet company or a fast food chain, and ask them what they are doing to make healthy snacks.
- Do a screen grab of any replies.